RAF AIRCRAFT OF THE BATTLE OF

A PHOTOGRAPHIC GUIDE TO SURVIVING PLANES

LEE CHAPMAN

Foreword by Squadron Leader Mark Discombe AFC &
Sqn Leader Mandy Singleton PG Dip, BEng (Hons) CEng

KEY

Acknowledgements

The author and publisher would like to thank the following organisations for permission to use copyright material in this book: the Shuttleworth Collection, the Imperial War Museum, the RAF Museum and the Midland Air Museum for permissions to photograph their exhibits on their sites. The Spirit of Britain re-enactors helped to bring some of the images to life, permission to use photographs featuring them is greatly appreciated. Every attempt has been made to seek permissions for copyright material and photographic rights in this book. However, if we have inadvertently used materials without permission we apologise, and we will make the necessary correction at the first opportunity.

The author would also like to thank Georgia Massey for all her support and patience, Keith Chapman and Andy 'Loopy' Forester for joining him on many aircraft photography adventures. He would also like to acknowledge the support given to him from the team at Battle of Britain Memorial Flight who provided the foreword to this book. The author would also like to credit Ian Grigg for his support and for many of the photographic opportunities that he has helped to provide through Airscene. The author would also like to thank all the air show organisers, warbird operators, restorers, conservators and museum curators that keep the memories alive. Finally, he would like to thank Jonathan Jackson and the team at Key Publishing for giving him the chance to fulfil a lifelong ambition of producing a published book.

Author's Note

The author has tried to document as many of the surviving Battle of Britain aircraft as possible, and while it was not possible to photograph every one, this book seeks to provide examples of all the aircraft types that played a significant role in the battle. It deliberately includes a small number of other aircraft, such as the training and bombing aircraft which, while not participants in the Battle of Britain, were an indispensable part of the RAF effort that enabled victory in 1940. Occasionally, the author has also included later or alternate marks of aircraft that were not active during 1940 to demonstrate where similar types can be seen today.

Published by Key Books
An imprint of Key Publishing Ltd
PO Box 100
Stamford
Lincs PE19 1XQ

www.keypublishing.com

The right of Lee Chapman to be identified as the author of this book has been asserted in accordance with the Copyright, Designs and Patents Act 1988 Sections 77 and 78.

Copyright © Lee Chapman, 2020

ISBN 978 1 913295 82 0

20 21 22 23 24   10 9 8 7 6 5 4 3 2 1

Typeset by Aura Technology and Software Services, India.

CONTENTS

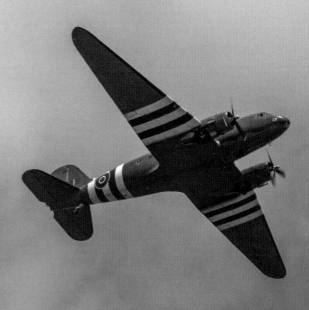

The Battle of Britain Memorial Flight's Dakota, Lancaster, Spitfire and Hurricane perform for the RAF100 celebrations in 2018.

FOREWORD

As a serving Royal Air Force pilot there is nothing that can prepare you for your first flight in one of the most iconic fighters in the world. The Hurricane and Spitfire represent not just the herculean technical achievements of the British aerospace industry at the time but also the country's struggle against evil, with the Battle of Britain being one of the first of many turning points against Nazi aggression. The background of these aircraft hangs heavy on any pilot during their first flight; for those flying with the Battle of Britain Memorial Flight (BBMF) this would initially be in the Hurricane and eventually in the Spitfire. In the modern RAF, all first flights come after extensive simulator and/or twin-seat training. However, for the BBMF pilot, like our forebears, there is no such comfort blanket. The differences between the two types were eloquently and accurately described by the late Squadron Leader Geoffrey Wellum DFC: 'The Hurricane is a workhorse and the Spitfire a thoroughbred!' Certainly, the Hurricane takes a little more to get going but she is more forgiving of less than perfect landings. However, she can bounce like a balloon. The Spitfire flies as though she was from another generation, feeling part of you and responding effortlessly to your inputs. Following the path of the BBMF's training, the unknowns that shock the most seasoned pilot in the Hurricane are removed when they first fly a Spitfire, allowing more time to marvel in their privileged position. Simply put, your first flight in a Hurricane is an assault on the senses; your first flight in a Spitfire is an assault on the emotions.

Squadron Leader Mark Discombe AFC
Officer Commanding the RAF Battle of Britain Memorial Flight

For an aero-systems engineer within the Royal Air Force, being the Senior Engineering Officer of the iconic Battle of Britain Memorial Flight is a privilege and an honour. Being responsible for maintaining and operating the breadth of aircraft types and marks to modern airworthiness standards is a daily challenge that brings with it frustrations that are only matched by the joy of hearing the aircraft engines start up and seeing them taxi by. The resourcefulness required to maintain these priceless aircraft using libraries full of diagrams and drawings dating back to the 1940s, which are often incomplete with hand-written amendments, astounds me daily. The team undertake everything from fabric repairs and maintaining piston engines to sensitively modifying the aircraft and installing modern safety equipment, such as modern radios. The BBMF's small team of highly skilled engineers are dedicated to keeping the authenticity and personality of every aircraft. They love, cherish and maintain them to the highest of standards, ensuring their preservation for future generations and for many years to come.

Sqn Leader Mandy Singleton PG Dip, BEng (Hons), CEng
Senior Engineering Officer for the RAF Battle of Britain Memorial Flight

The Imperial War Museum's Supermarine
Spitfire Mk Ia, N3200.

PREFACE

The Battle of Britain is widely considered to be Britain's finest hour. At the time of writing there is only one surviving pilot who fought during the conflict. The 'Few' will not be forgotten, nor will they be around forever to recount the heroism of the summer of 1940 first-hand. In contrast, the number of restored and preserved aircraft in our museums and skies is at an all-time high. Authentic warbirds have never been better cared for in our museums and formations of over 15 Spitfires and half a dozen Hurricanes are not unheard of at UK air shows. It is now left to the sights and sounds of these surviving aircraft to remind us of the sacrifices, daring and bravery of those who saved Britain from imminent invasion in 1940.

This book features a brief history of the wide range of RAF aircraft that were involved in the famous battle. As well as exploring the key fighters and bombers, some of the major training and support aeroplanes that contributed to the iconic events have also been included. The story will be told using images of surviving and restored aircraft in the air and on the ground, including photographs of them in unique formations together.

The images have been drawn from the author's personal collection. As a media photographer and keen enthusiast, over the last ten years he has visited many airfields, attended many air shows, flypasts and museum events. He has been fortunate to get up close and photograph aircraft representative of many of the types used during the period. Some of the images that feature in the book include airframes with genuine Battle of Britain experience. Where this is not possible, similar aircraft types have been used as a representation; occasionally, later marks and models have been included to complete the story.

The author has attempted to take a wider look at the aircraft used during the battle as there were many aircraft types that played a role during the Battle of Britain. Every attempt has been made to include as many significant aircraft across different sectors as possible. Any decisions to include or omit aircraft have also been led by modern-day availability. Considerable research into the period has been conducted; numbers, dates, facts and figures often vary in different sources, but every attempt has been made to reflect history accurately.

The *Spirit of Britain* re-enactors head towards
Supermarine Spitfire Mk Ia, N3200.

CHAPTER 1
INTRODUCTION

The Battle of Britain was an aerial conflict fought between the months of July and October in 1940. Adolf Hitler's Germany had already taken most of Western Europe and had formed plans to invade the United Kingdom. Before Operation *Sealion* could commence, the destruction of the Royal Air Force in the air and on the ground was ordered. Some 3,000 Allied aircrew took part in the battle, many of them foreign volunteers drawn from the British Empire, the Commonwealth and the occupied countries of Europe.

In a rare formation, the world's only surviving airworthy Bristol Blenheim leads three Mk Ia Spitfires, five Hawker Hurricanes and a Gloster Gladiator. The authentic sound of several Rolls-Royce Merlin and Bristol Mercury engines passing overhead is enough to stir the emotions and remind all of the sacrifices made by the pilots and aircrew during the summer of 1940.

When Hitler started his campaign to invade the low countries in central Europe it is widely believed that he did not expect Britain to put up much resistance. Hitler did not see Britain as an enemy, although once war was declared an attempted invasion of Britain was inevitable. Following on from the Dunkirk evacuation, the military leaders of Nazi Germany felt that Britain was defeated, and an immediate paratrooper invasion could take place. Hitler stalled and ordered the destruction of the RAF before the invasion could commence.

Although the heroic deeds of 1940 have achieved immortal status there are few survivors left from the conflict to tell the tale first-hand. However, 80 years on many enthusiasts have dedicated considerable time and resources to the protection, preservation and restoration of surviving aircraft and equipment. In a scene reminiscent of the period, modern-day re-enactors from the *Spirit of Britain* group wait beside their Hawker Hurricane for a squadron scramble.

The Luftwaffe would be tasked with clearing the way for invasion, and the plan was for a full-scale aerial attack to commence on 'Eagle Day'. Hermann Göring would lead his air force into battle, believing that the conflict would be over in two to three weeks. After all, he was aware of his superior aircraft numbers having over 1,400 bombers, 320 long-range Bf 110 fighters and over 800 single-seater fighters. As the battle raged on, a small Italian fleet of aircraft known as the Corpo Aereo Italiano also entered the conflict in support of Hitler's Germany.

Today, genuine German-built aircraft from this period are rare, but the Spanish-built version of the Bf 109, the Hispano Buchón, has often played this role at air shows and in the famous 1969 *Battle of Britain* film. Air Leasing Ltd have recently restored a number of Hispano Buchóns, three of which appear here with the Aircraft Restoration Company's 'Yellow 10'. The Fighter Collection at Duxford are also working hard restoring a (Swedish-built) Fiat CR.42 to represent the Italian connection.

destruction and heartache, it is little wonder that not much thought was given over to the preservation of now redundant weapons of war. The advent of the jet age and the atomic bomb made war-weary piston-fighters particularly out-dated. As such, very few of the planes that saved Britain remained airworthy by the 1950s. The filming of the 1969 film, *Battle of Britain*, reversed their fortunes and kickstarted the now booming warbird movement. Today, sights like this Mk Ia Spitfire escorted by two Hawker Hurricanes are not uncommon in English skies during the summer months.

A delay to Eagle Day allowed the British aircraft industry to find its feet and start mass-producing its much-needed fighters. Most people will be familiar with the famous role that the Supermarine Spitfire played during the Battle of Britain. Although less glamourous, the Hawker Hurricane is almost as equally well recognised for its contribution to the battle. In July 1940, the RAF had only around 200 Spitfires, 350 Hurricanes and a small number of other largely obsolete or unsuitable fighters to defend against the onslaught.

At the end of the Second World War thoughts were turned towards recovery and reparation and away from war. After five years of hardship,

Over 20 squadrons of Spitfires played a role in the air war over Britain in the summer of 1940. The spitfire was continually improved and upgraded to keep pace with the development of German fighters. More often than not, the latest Spitfire was more than a match for its nearest rival in the Luftwaffe. Production of Spitfires during the war remained high and generally matched or exceeded losses. However, early marks of Spitfire, like those that fought in the Battle of Britain, are rare and precious today.

Organisations such as the Aircraft Restoration Company, Air Leasing Ltd, the Fighter Collection, Airframes Assemblies, the Biggin Hill Heritage Hangar, Historic Aircraft Collection and Hawker Restorations are ensuring that the efforts of the designers, engineers and aircrew from 1940 remain as living exhibits so that new generations can see the sights and sense the sounds and smells of the Battle of Britain. Eighty years on, it is possible to see more Spitfires, Hurricanes and other warbirds in our skies than at any other point since the end of the war.

A flight of 14 aircraft made up of 13 Supermarine Spitfires and a Supermarine Seafire (a naval version of the Spitfire).

The Spitfire and Hurricane were far from the only aircraft types to contribute to the effort to repel the Luftwaffe and prevent a full-blown German invasion. Other fighters, such as the Boulton Paul Defiant and Gloster Gladiator, were also on the front line at the start of the battle. Fighters alone were not enough to win the war. Pilots needed to learn and refine their skills in aircraft such as the de Havilland Tiger Moth. Strategists needed data from aerial reconnaissance and the war effort required numerous transport and support aircraft to keep the wheels turning.

Although some of the types of the period did not stand the tests of time, we are fortunate that, despite the odds, several significant airframes remain airworthy or on public display. Keeping an 80-year-old aeroplane in the skies does not come without sacrifice. In the interests of safety, it is often essential to replace authentic components with modern-day copies and in some cases re-design or rebuild significant aspects of an airframe or engine.

The UK is fortunate to have not just an ever-growing population of flying memorials, but also a rich, authentic and pure collection of museum pieces from the period. These are expertly cared for and lovingly preserved in a vast network of aviation museums up and down the country.

It's hard to separate the stories of the men and women from the aircraft that they helped to design, build, deliver, maintain and fly in the fight against tyranny during the Second World War. It was, after all, the people who fought the war and not the machines. There are countless books that examine the individual contributions of brave pilots, innovative designers and tireless engineers. Without their efforts we would not be remembering the aircraft now.

Despite all that was going on, the pilots and engineers in the Battle of Britain were still able to marvel and wonder at the aircraft in their charge, just as we do today. Although the aircraft are no longer the cutting-edge technology they were in 1940, they still turn heads wherever they go. The sleek lines of the Spitfire still look fresh and clean, the Hurricane still appears menacing, poised on the ground like a British Bulldog, and the Westland Lysander can still amaze with its tight take-offs and landings.

North American Harvard KF183. This aircraft was only retired from military service in 2016, having been operated for over 72 years in total, with over 60 years' service for QinetiQ.

CHAPTER 2

PREPARING FOR BATTLE: TRAINING AIRCRAFT

At the outbreak of the war, flight training in the Royal Air Force was organised into three stages: Elementary, Service Flight and Operational training. New recruits would get to grips with basic flight controls during Elementary Flying Training, and after around 50 hours on types such as the de Havilland Tiger Moth, budding pilots would be ready to move on to the next stage. Service Flight Training had two aspects: Initial and Advanced training. Recruits would amass another 100 hours here on more powerful aircraft, including the Miles Master and North American Harvard. The final stage for the budding fighter pilot would be the Operational Training Unit where pilots could hone their skills on the front-line fighters for a further 40 hours.

Both fighter and bomber pilots would follow a similar regime, albeit with different aircraft – for example, twin-engine aircraft specialists would cut their teeth on the Airspeed Oxford rather than the single-engine Miles Magister. As the Battle of Britain progressed, the shortage of front-line pilots became a real concern and the training programme was condensed into a shorter timeframe. The urgent need for pilots also led to a somewhat eclectic range of aircraft being used at the various training schools. Relics such as the Avro Tutor and impressed civilian aeroplanes were put to good use when the more standard types were not available.

A Miles Magister, Avro Tutor and de Havilland Tiger Moth displaying together at one of the Shuttleworth Collection's air shows.

When a fresh-faced recruit arrived on his first day of flight training, he would be presented with a rugged biplane to use to begin his quest to conquer the skies. After a few weeks of ground instruction, pilots would be allowed to take control of their first aircraft. For the majority, this would be the de Havilland Tiger Moth (pictured in the background). However, the urgent need for new pilots led to a range of other types being utilised, and even some civilian flying schools were used.

The Avro Tutor (pictured in the foreground) was a two-seater radial engine trainer. It was developed during the late 1920s as a metal replacement for the wooden, ageing Avro 504. It was quickly adopted by the RAF as their main primary trainer. Over 400 were taken on charge from 1933, and over 200 remained in service when the war broke out.

The Avro 621 Tutor was designed in 1929 by Roy Chadwick, who would later design the Lancaster and Vulcan. The aircraft was built using a metal welded tube construction with a fabric covering. The early examples were fitted with Armstrong-Siddeley Mongoose radial engines, but later they were upgraded to the more powerful Lynx powerplant.

This aircraft (K3215) was one of only three Tutors to survive the war and the only Tutor that remains today. It is owned and operated by the Shuttleworth Collection in Old Warden, Bedfordshire. K3215 saw service with the RAF College Cranwell and the Central Flying School, where it remained in service as a communications aircraft throughout the war. Sadly, a crankshaft failure during filming prevented the Tutor from performing its planned role in the Douglas Bader biopic, *Reach for the Sky*. Today, the aircraft is still airworthy and operates the only working Armstrong-Siddeley Lynx engine anywhere in the world. It currently poses as K3241 in the colours of the Central Flying School's Aerobatic team.

The de Havilland DH 82 Tiger Moth was designed by Geoffrey de Havilland in the early 1930s. It was the mainstay of Royal Air Force primary training during the Battle of Britain. As well as giving most pilots their first flying experience, the Tiger Moth was also used as a maritime reconnaissance aircraft and some were even kitted out as light bombers!

The DH 82 was a development of the already successful DH 60 Gipsy Moth which had been a popular civilian tourer. The new Tiger Moth had been given an inverted Gipsy III or Gipsy Major engine which greatly improved the forward view, ideal for the excited, trembling recruit as he taxied out for the first time. This particular Tiger Moth (T6818) was built by Morris Motors in 1944 and now flies regularly for the Shuttleworth Trust based in Old Warden, Bedfordshire.

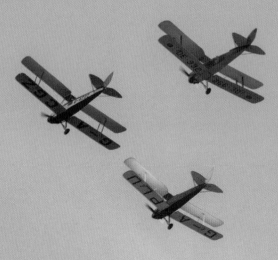

The Tiger Moth entered service in the RAF Central Flying School in 1932 and would go on serving in the RAF as its basic trainer until the 1950s. Its docile flying characteristics made it ideal for thousands of future front-line pilots to get their first taste of flying.

Today, over 250 de Havilland Tiger Moths are thought to be airworthy, and there are also numerous examples in museums all over the world. The Tiger Nine Aerobatic Display Team often appear at UK air shows with their unique formation of nine Tiger Moths. On this occasion, the team, led by Jeff Milsom in G-AHOO, comprised eight Tiger Moths and one Moth Major.

The success of the de Havilland Tiger Moth design led to several variants and spin-offs. One notable version was the DH 82B Queen Bee, a pilotless, radio-controlled version of the popular trainer. The aircraft was known as a 'drone' in reference to the male bee, which makes one flight in search of its queen. Thus, this aircraft was the first drone in the Royal Air Force. From 1935 onwards, the Queen Bee was used to help train the anti-aircraft gunners, whose role in the protection of Great Britain during the battle cannot be underestimated.

Despite its wooden structure and somewhat hazardous occupation, there are still two surviving Queen Bees in the UK. One can be found at the de Havilland Aircraft Museum in London and the other, LF858, is still airworthy and based at RAF Henlow, Bedfordshire. LF858 has now been fitted with full flying controls in the rear cockpit and often performs balloon popping and aerial stunts as part of Captain Neville's Flying Circus.

To fill gaps in aircraft availability and flight training, many civilian aircraft were impressed into RAF service. The Blackburn B-2 was not successful in gaining any major military contracts but, nevertheless, some 42 were built and populated Blackburn-owned civilian training schools at Brough Aerodrome and London Air Park. These civilian schools made themselves busy training pilots on behalf of the Royal Air Force.

As war was declared in 1939, the aircraft were merged into one flight school and became the No. 4 Elementary Flying Training School. The aircraft remained civilian initially but were given the RAF training colour scheme of the time. Today, only one airworthy Blackburn B-2 survives, G-AEBJ, which is now owned by BAE Systems as part of their heritage flight based out of Old Warden.

After 'going solo' and building up 25 hours during Elementary Flying Training, student pilots would progress to the first stage of Service Flight Training. Here, the young men would receive much-needed experience on different aircraft, more like those on the front line. Front-line fighters were considerably more powerful than the likes of the Tiger Moth and were predominantly monoplanes with enclosed cockpits. Recruits would look to progress towards cutting-edge fighting machines via basic and advanced trainers.

The Miles M.14 Magister was a two-seater aeroplane that served as a basic trainer in the Royal Air Force. As a low-winged monoplane it made an ideal introduction to the world of the Hurricane and Spitfire. The Magister first took flight in 1937, and just two years later the RAF was equipped with over 700 of them.

The new generation of high-performance monoplane fighters in the RAF, such as the Spitfire and Hurricane, created a gap in the Air Force's training syllabus. The Air Ministry deemed it necessary to commission a suitable monoplane trainer. The Miles Magister was the first aircraft to fulfil this role. The Miles aircraft company also produced the Miles Master as a very successful advanced trainer for the RAF, but sadly no complete examples of this type remain.

This magister was registered as V1075 in the RAF, where it served until 1942. V1075 has passed through several owners. It was restored to flight in 1990 and is now owned by one of the Shuttleworth Collection's pilots, David Bramwell. It is based at Old Warden Aerodrome.

The Miles Aircraft Company developed the Magister from their civilian Hawk Major and Hawk Trainer. It proved a step up from the Tiger Moth but retained the fixed undercarriage and open cockpit; it was also powered by a Gipsy Major engine. Generally considered a successful second phase trainer by the RAF, many of the airframes were adopted for air racing after the war.

P6382 was built in 1939 and served with the RAF during the war. Due to the delicate plywood structure, the whole of the aircraft did not stand the tests of time. The Shuttleworth Collection apprentices were able to utilise components of three other Magisters to produce this airworthy example. It now makes up one of only a handful of airworthy Magisters left in the world.

Not all front-line Battle of Britain pilots would be lucky enough to fly the iconic Spitfire. Many would progress down the twin-engine route towards the Bristol Beaufighter or Blenheim. To meet training needs for all twin-engine types, including both fighters and bombers, the RAF utilised the Airspeed Oxford. This versatile aeroplane permitted the training of the complete aircrew, including navigators, radio operators, gunners, bomb-aimers and pilots. Other aircraft, such as the de Havilland Dominie, were also used to help train navigators. During the Battle of Britain most of these were civilian aircraft drafted in for military use.

The Oxford was produced by Airspeed in response to an Air Ministry request. It was developed from their already successful Envoy. Thousands

Classic Wing's de Havilland Dominie, TX310. The Dominie was known as the Dragon Rapide in civilian hands.

of Oxfords were produced and put into service by Britain and its allies, and the 'Ox-Box', as it was known, remained in service with the RAF until 1956. This example, V3388, is currently hanging from the ceiling in IWM Duxford's Airspace hangar. V3388 is one of only two Oxfords currently on display in the UK; there are no airworthy examples left. There are over ten airworthy Dominies surviving in the UK, and you can even take pleasure flights in some of these.

As tensions developed across Europe, the Royal Air Force turned to America to acquire aircraft to equip its new Empire Training Scheme. Several North American Harvard's were delivered to the UK, but many were sent to Commonwealth Countries safe from the conflict, such as Canada and Southern Rhodesia, where pilots could hone their skills in relative safety.

There are several Harvards/Texans still intact in the world today, and many of these remain airworthy, including over 35 in the UK alone. Even more remarkably, many are still in use as an advanced trainer to allow modern pilots to gain much needed experience as they step up to the more powerful historic warbirds such as the Supermarine Spitfire.

Over 17,000 North American Harvards were built during the Second World War. Approximately 5,000 of these were sent to British and Commonwealth Air Forces. The Harvard was known as the Texan in the USA and, along with the Miles Master, was one of the RAF's go-to advanced trainers. After graduating from basic training types, pilots would receive their 'wings', but they would need to gain a further 50 hours on the advanced trainers before being deemed fit to polish off their skills on one of the front-line fighters.

G-BJST is actually a Harvard IV that was built in 1953 in Canada. However, in 2014 it was decided that it would be given the markings of AJ841, a Desert Air Force Harvard. The 'Wacky Wabbit' nose art was not known to be on any aircraft of the time but was taken from a patch used by the No. 5 British Flying Training School, which was based in Florida during the war.

The Shuttleworth Collection's Westland Lysander.

CHAPTER 3

BOMBERS AND SUPPORT AIRCRAFT

The traditional view of the Battle of Britain is centred directly around home defence, and the glamour and chivalry of the front-line fighter, which means supporting roles are often overlooked. The key turning point of the conflict is often cited as when the German bombers switched targets away from airfields and towards the cities. This was in retaliation to the British bombing raids over Germany, which is surely reason enough to include the bombers as honorary Battle of Britain aircraft. On top of that, when the fighters needed direction, vital reconnaissance came from Coastal Command patrols – Westland Lysanders patrolling British skies from dawn till dusk, watching and waiting. The Spitfire and

Hurricane were certainly instrumental in the postponement of the German invasion, but they did not do it alone.

Surviving early Second World War bombers are rare beasts, and except for the sole Bristol Blenheim (leading this formation) none remain in airworthy condition. A few examples of period twin-engine bombers remain intact in museums but, sadly, not all types made it. The Aircraft Restoration Company's newly restored Westland Lysander has doubled the number of 'Lizzies' flying in the UK. The two supporting aircraft can be seen here behind the Blenheim. The Gloster Gladiator makes up the final plane in this Bristol Mercury engine flypast.

The Avro Anson served in the Royal Air Force for over 30 years, its prolonged reliability earning it the nickname 'Faithful Annie'. Almost 400 Ansons directly contributed to Britain's air defences during the Battle of Britain, through RAF Coastal Command. The Anson saw a varied career in the Royal Air Force, but during the heat of the Battle of Britain eight squadrons were tasked with protecting British shipping lanes. At this point, the Faithful Annies were beginning to show their age and were steadily replaced by Lockheed Hudsons from America.

This Anson, a Mk I, was built at the Newton Heath Avro factory in 1938. It served during the Battle of Britain with the Air Transport Auxiliary as part of the Ferry Pilots Pool. It is currently on display in the Airspace hangar at IWM Duxford, where it proudly wears the markings of Pilot Officer P. W. Peters, who shot down two enemy aircraft over Kent in his Anson on 1 June 1940.

Although the Avro Anson would continue to serve with the RAF well after the war, its weaknesses as a front-line aircraft were quickly noted during the Battle of Britain. The Ansons of Coastal Command were considerably slower than their German counterparts and as such needed to be replaced. Rather than waste a reliable airframe, the remaining aircraft were either shipped abroad to help establish the Empire training schemes or transferred to transport or support roles within the RAF.

In the UK, there are two airworthy Avro Anson's flying. G-AHKX is part of the BAE Systems heritage flight and operates alongside the Shuttleworth Collection at Old Warden. This is a later development of the Anson. Built for the civilian market as an Avro XIX, it has recently been repainted to military markings, but can be seen over the page in its former civilian markings. The, now privately owned, WD413 did serve with the RAF in the 1950s and was later converted to passenger configuration and designated a C.21.

The Vickers-Armstrong Wellington was designed by Dr Barnes Wallis (of bouncing-bomb Dambusters fame), with the prototype making its first flight on 15 June 1936. During the early stages of the war, the Wellington did not fare well against German fighters. Many modifications, including additional protection, self-sealing fuel tanks and redesigned hydraulics, led to an aircraft that would play a major part in bombing and reconnaissance until the four-engine heavies took over those duties in the middle of the war. During the Battle of Britain, eight squadrons of Wellingtons were available and carried out missions on enemy targets almost every day of the conflict. German fighters continued to get the better of the bomber until it was switched to night operations in August 1940.

The Royal Air Force had a trio of twin-engine bombers at their disposal during the Battle of Britain. The last of these to enter service was the Handley Page Hampden. Around 700 of these were built but over half were lost on operations. The Hampden was the most active of the three primary bombers during the battle, and seven squadrons took several missions, day and night, deep into enemy territory.

Very few Battle of Britain period bombers have survived, though two are presently undergoing conservation work at the RAF Museum. Hampden I, P1344, was recovered from a crash site in Russia in 1991 and it will soon be on display at Hendon, initially without its wings. Vickers Wellington MF628 is a T.10 variant that is currently in a striped-down state but will soon be returned to display. There is currently just one other Wellington bomber, a Mk Ia on display at Brooklands Museum. There are no other Hampdens viewable but two long-term projects, one in Canada and the other in Lincolnshire, could see this rectified.

The Armstrong Whitworth Whitley was the first aircraft called into action during the Second World War when it was tasked with dropping thousands of notelets over Germany on the very first day. Six squadrons of Whitleys undertook bombing raids daily during the months of the Battle of Britain. The twin Merlin-engined bomber was always designed as a night-time bomber, but when the Halifax and Lancaster took over this role the Whitley would continue to serve as a glider tug and paratrooper training aeroplane.

Despite its historic importance, no complete examples of the Armstrong Whitworth Whitley remain. The recovered wreckage of N1498 is currently on display at the Midlands Air Museum, Coventry, a location very close to where it was built. This is currently the most substantial Whitley on display, but the Midland Aircraft Recovery Group are also salvaging various crash remains in the hope of one day reviving the type.

Designed for Army Co-operation, the Westland Lysander entered RAF service in 1938, and was initially used for message dropping and artillery spotting. During the Battle for France, Lysanders were also required for light-bombing and spotting duties. The 'Lizzie', as it was known, was not well suited to such roles as its slow speed made it vulnerable to the Luftwaffe. Later in the war, it would find its niche as a special operations aircraft as short take-off and landing capabilities made it ideal for collecting and dropping off special agents behind enemy lines.

During the Battle of Britain, Westland Lysanders flew dawn and dusk patrols off the British coast in search of invaders. Should an invasion of Britain have taken place, the nine squadrons of Lizzies were ready to attack the landing beaches with a barrage of light bombs and machine-gun fire. Fortunately, this service was not required. Four Lysanders remain intact in the UK today; two of these are airworthy.

Even at the height of the Battle of Britain, the Westland Lysander was being prepared for its defining role. No. 419 Flight, based at North Weald, began using the Lysander to convey and retrieve covert agents from France. Other Lysanders were used in a search-and-rescue role, and most fighter squadrons had one on stand-by, ready to search for surviving crew forced to ditch.

Westland Lysander V9312 (G-CCOM) is owned and operated by the Aircraft Restoration Company, who spent several years painstakingly restoring it to airworthy status. It is thought to be the only true 'Westland' Lysander remaining; all remaining others have several Canadian components incorporated into their re-builds. It was built during 1940 but did not enter service until after the Battle of Britain. It is, however, currently painted in the livery of No. 225 Squadron, who were heavily involved in operations in the summer of 1940.

August 1940 saw the beginning of the delivery of the newly refined Mk IIIA Lysanders. They were armed with twin guns in the rear cockpit and given self-sealing fuel tanks and an uprated, more powerful engine. Despite this, it was obvious that this was not going to be an aircraft capable of holding its own against German fighters; the Lysander's strengths lay elsewhere.

Westland Lysander V9552 was originally built for the RAF but was sent to Canada in 1942 to operate as a target tug for the RCAF. Since 1999, it has been operated by the Shuttleworth Collection as V9367, a Mk III Lysander from No. 161 Squadron. The aircraft appears in its night-time markings as used by the Special Duties Unit from RAF Tempsford. The rasping sound of its 870hp Bristol Mercury XX engine can still be heard overhead at the majority of the air shows at Old Warden throughout the summer.

At the beginning of the Battle of Britain, 18 squadrons of Lysanders were operational but, for a variety of reasons, this was cut to 12 by September. Despite their readiness and continued operations of varying nature throughout the battle, only one Lysander was involved in a shoot-out with an enemy aircraft, resulting in neither side sustaining significant damage.

Suspended from the ceiling in the impressive Airspace hangar at IWM Duxford, V9300 was built during the Battle of Britain and was one of the first newly updated Mk IIIAs. It entered service with the RAF just after the battle had ceased and as such was packed up as part of the spare aircraft pool, before being shipped to Canada a year later. Restoration of one other Lysander (R9125) has just been completed and it will soon be on display at the RAF Museum.

Also seen here, is the enormous Shorts Sunderland flying boat. This was nicknamed the Flying Porcupine by the Germans due to its impressive defensive armament. During the Battle of Britain, the huge flying boats were almost constantly out, undertaking long missions in often challenging conditions. Despites its lumbering size, the Sunderland was a surprisingly effective foe against the Luftwaffe aircraft they would often encounter while on U-boat patrols.

Aircraft filled many roles during the Battle of Britain, the famous fighters and bombers are the ones that grab the headlines, but their jobs could not have been done without support. Transport of air crew, engineers and equipment was vital in keeping the front-line airfields replenished. In the first half of the Battle of Britain, airfields were specifically targeted by the Luftwaffe, killing and injuring personnel and destroying equipment and aircraft on the ground as well as in the air.

To fulfil some of these roles, many civilian aircraft were impressed into Royal Air Force service. For example, aircraft like the de Havilland Rapide (the Dominie in RAF service) were useful for transporting crew, the Fairchild Argus was a rugged communications aircraft capable of landing on rough airfields and, finally, the de Havilland Hornet Moth performed several roles, including liaison. This example (WD385) was used by No. 3 Coastal Patrol Flight in 1940 to look out for and scare U-boats into diving.

There are several de Havilland Rapides/Dominies still flying today. NR808 was built in 1945 and allocated to the British military but is now restored in genuine British European Airways colours. Dominie X7344 was built for the RAF in 1941 but registered to Scottish Airways in October 1943. It is now preserved in wartime camouflage.

Communication was another challenge in 1940 as messages via radio were easily intercepted. Liaison aircraft could ferry important orders and transport high commanding officers to confidential meetings and small, light aircraft such as the Fairchild Argus fulfilled these roles. The contribution of supporting aircraft to the war effort cannot be underestimated.

Fairchild Argus III KK527 was built in 1944 and taken on charge with the RAF until 1949. It was far too late to take a role during the Battle of Britain, but it is visually similar to earlier Argus aircraft used during 1940. It has passed through several owners and colour schemes but appears here in British Army markings.

The Shuttleworth Collection's Gloster Gladiator.

CHAPTER 4

BIPLANE LEGACY

During the 1930s, the Royal Air Force operated a series of very attractive silver biplanes. At the outbreak of the Second World War, some of these remained in service, with those in the firing line being hastily re-painted in a more sensible, but less striking, camouflage scheme. Some of these, such as the Gloster Gladiator, even found themselves on the front line during the Battle of Britain. Other types would have been relegated to transport and training roles as the battle commenced.

This image shows a trio of Hawker Biplanes in formation, with the Hawker Demon leading two Hawker Nimrods. The Hawker Nimrod was the naval equivalent of the Hawker Fury. Incredibly, the remains of two Nimrods were found in a scrap yard in West London during the 1970s and they were donated to the RAF Museum, who eventually passed them on for restoration to flight. S1581 is now operated by the Fighter Collection and K3661 is operated by the Historic Aircraft Collection. Both remaining Nimrods are based at IWM Duxford.

The Gloster SS 37 (Gladiator) prototype was first tested in July 1935 at Martlesham Heath, where it reached speeds of over 250mph, 40mph faster than the current RAF fighter planes. However, it was already obsolete by 30 October that year when the Hawker Hurricane made its maiden flight. Despite this, Gladiators still fought gallantly in the early part of the war, operating in Norway from a frozen lake and undertaking several missions during the Battle for France.

Thanks to the creativity of the organisers of the Shuttleworth Collection's air shows we can compare the Hawker Hurricane (R4118) and the Gloster Gladiator (L8032) as they fly together. The Gladiator features a metal frame, powerful Bristol Mercury radial engine and, for the first time on an RAF biplane, an enclosed cockpit. The retracting undercarriage and missing top wing section would help to reduce drag and enhance performance in the more modern monoplane fighters.

The Hawker Hart was used as an advanced RAF trainer. It was developed from the bomber variant and was introduced in 1930. It was considered a great success – in fact, its performance exceeded that of many front-line fighters, which prompted the development of a fighter version. Some Harts were still in service at the beginning of the war; famous author and fighter pilot Roald Dahl would conduct his initial training in Iraq on the Hawker Hart. Battle of Britain ace, Tom Neil, remarked on how he felt at home during his first flight in the Hawker Hurricane having also trained on the Hart as many of its features were retained in Hawker's masterpiece. During the Battle of Britain, Harts were mainly relegated to communication and ground-instructional roles.

Many of the experienced Battle of Britain pilots will have cut their teeth on these iconic silver machines in the lead-up to the war. Even more critically, the manufacturing and design techniques used for them led to the development and production of the iconic monoplane fighters. The Hawker Hurricane, for example, shares a lot of traits with the preceding Hawker Hart family of biplanes.

K4872 is currently on display at the RAF Museum, Cosford. It was built in 1935 and served with several flight training schools during the build-up to the war. At the beginning of 1940, it was given a brand-new Kestrel engine but remained within the Maintenance Unit throughout the Battle of Britain. It was returned to use as a ground-instructional airframe in 1943.

The Hawker Fury served as a front-line fighter for the RAF between 1935 and 1939. It was the first RAF fighter to achieve speeds over 200mph and was considered ground-breaking at the time. By 1939, the Hawker Fury was removed from the RAF front line and replaced by Hurricanes and Gladiators. This was a wise move, as those that remained in service with foreign air arms were often unsuccessful against more sophisticated Luftwaffe aircraft; in 1941, the Yugoslav Air Force lost almost an entire Hawker Fury squadron in one German attack alone. The Fury remained in service with the RAF as a training aircraft during the Battle of Britain.

K5674 is the only airworthy Fury in the world and is operated by the Historic Aircraft Collection from IWM Duxford. It saw service with the RAF until 1939, at which point it was transferred to the South African Air Force where it was written off after a forced landing. After almost ten years under restoration, it flew again in 2012. One other Hawker Fury (K1928) is currently being restored by the Cambridge Bomber and Fighter Society at Little Gransden. Once complete this will go on display at Brooklands Museum.

The Hawker Demon was a two-seater fighter version of the Hart. When the Hawker Hart trainer entered RAF service it was noted that its performance outclassed that of the current single-seater fighters, such as the Bristol Bulldog. A super-charged kestrel engine and two Vickers machine guns were fitted, and the Demon was born. Over 300 Demons were built, with some remaining in service during the Battle of Britain, mostly as target tugs for training purposes

K8203 is operated by Demon Displays Limited from Old Warden, Bedfordshire. It was built by Boulton Paul in 1937 and served with the RAF later that year. After a 70-year break in flying, K8203 took to the skies once more in 2009. It is the only Demon in the UK, but one other is on display in Australia, where the Demon also served.

The Gloster Gladiator was the last of the RAF's biplane fighters. It performed well when it initially entered service in the mid-1930s. However, work was already well underway on more streamlined monoplanes that would soon bring an end to the days of the biplane. When the Battle of Britain began, supplies of the more modern fighters had not yet reached all units. No. 247 Squadron, based at RAF Roborough, near Devon, was still equipped with the ageing Gladiator.

One of the surviving Gladiators (L8032) now wears the colours of K7895, showing how the Gloster aeroplanes would have appeared in 1937. The silver biplanes were wisely given a hasty camouflaged scheme at the outbreak of war. L8032 is currently based at Old Warden, Bedfordshire, and makes up part of the world-famous Shuttleworth Collection. It is a regular flyer at Shuttleworth air shows and often forms up with other aircraft of the period.

On the evening of 28 October 1940, six Gladiators of No. 247 Squadron took off on their usual night-time patrol – these sorties had taken place every evening since the squadron formed at RAF Roborough on 13 August 1940. Though these flights were usually uneventful, that night would be different. Pilot Officer Winter, flying N5622, made the first and only interception in a Gladiator during the Battle of Britain. Taking on a Heinkel He 111 over Plymouth, the out-dated biplane was not able to make a significant impact on the German bomber, but perhaps the brave pilot did enough to deter it from its intended target.

Gloster Gladiator (L8032) wearing the colours of K7895.

Crucially, in an unsung role, Gladiators undertook two meteorological flights every day during the Battle of Britain. Operating out of Aldergrove in Northern Ireland and RAF Mildenhall in Suffolk, pilots would climb to height and record temperature and humidity, the data that could be used to prepare weather forecasts for the operational flying units. Other Gladiators were also used for advanced training in No. 6 Operational Training Unit until August 1940.

The Fighter Collection's Gladiator, N5903 (G-GLAD), is one of only two airworthy examples in the world and was amongst the last of the Mk II aircraft built in 1939. It briefly served with No. 141 Squadron at Grangemouth, near Edinburgh, but was put into storage during the Battle of Britain. N5903 was used for training and ground instruction later in the war and was eventually put on display at the Fleet Air Museum in Yeovilton, before being returned to flight in 2008.

The only other complete Gladiator in the UK is currently on display at the RAF Museum, Cosford. The airframe makes up part of a Battle of Britain 80th Anniversary exhibition at the Shropshire site. During the Battle, this aircraft was held in storage at No. 5 MU in Kemble. It was later used for research and development. Along with the Shuttleworth Collection's example, it was used for filming an unfinished documentary in 1943 called *Signed with Their Honour*.

Although biplanes still had a role to play, the performance of monoplane fighters made them obsolete for front-line duties. The image here shows the dramatic difference in aerodynamics between the Gladiator biplane and three Supermarine Spitfires. The rapid advancement of German fighters made it far too hazardous to keep the likes of the Gloster Gladiator in harm's way as other European Air Arms had already seen their outdated biplane fighters crushed by the Luftwaffe. The outcome of the Battle of Britain would be determined by its monoplane fighters.

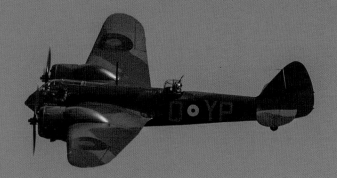

CHAPTER 5

FRONT-LINE FIGHTERS: BLENHEIM, BEAUFIGHTER AND DEFIANT

At the outset of the Battle of Britain, the Royal Air Force had several different fighter aircraft at its disposal. Air Chief Marshall Hugh Dowding was aware of the superiority of his Spitfires and Hurricanes, but also practical enough to make good use of what he had at his fingertips. In July 1940, Fighter Command had several squadrons of Bristol Blenheims, two squadrons of Boulton Paul Defiants and one squadron of Gloster Gladiators at its disposal. Bristol Beaufighters were on the production line and would be operational by August.

This image shows the Bristol Blenheim escorted by two Mk I Supermarine Spitfires. The Blenheim was a versatile aircraft that was also used as a light bomber, but its performance as a fighter could not match the speed or agility of the Spitfire.

formation attacks, which it successfully accomplished during the Battle for France. Thirty-seven enemy aircraft were claimed by Defiants for none in return on 29 May 1940 alone.

The Battle of France may have belonged to the Defiant, but the Battle of Britain would be tragically different. On 19 July 1940, 12 Defiants from the newly operational No. 141 Squadron were scrambled to face a swarm of Bf 109s. The Luftwaffe pilots were able to use their superior speed and swing to get the better of the squadron. Ten RAF aircrew would lose their lives and only two Defiants would return home. Following this incident, all operational Defiant squadrons were posted north to re-group away from the front line.

After a month's respite, No. 264 Squadron were called back into the action. They claimed nine German aircraft for the loss of four of theirs on the 24 August 1940. Two days later, they intercepted a wave of Do 17s, six of which were destroyed for the loss of three Defiants. Following the loss of another four Defiants on 28 August, the RAF's last turret fighter would be realigned to a night-fighting role. It was generally considered that two crew members were a real advantage for spotting enemy aircraft in the dark.

The Boulton Paul Defiant was a two-seater turret fighter aeroplane that has received mixed reviews over the years. Despite this, it remained a firm favourite amongst its crews. Its combat record speaks for itself – 152 victories against 37 loses, a good ratio for any aircraft during the Second World War. The Defiant was designed to undertake coordinated

Only one Boulton Paul Defiant has survived intact and can be seen at the RAF Museum in Cosford. It is currently on display alongside its Battle of Britain brothers, the Gladiator, Hurricane and Spitfire. The remaining example was taken on RAF charge at the height of the conflict in August 1940. It served with No. 307 (Polish) Squadron but was not fully operational until December of that year. It continued to serve until 1942, but by April 1944, it had already been set aside for preservation, even before the war had ended! The aircraft still wears the markings of No. 307 Squadron today.

The Bristol Blenheim was initially designed as an airliner in the 1930s as part of a project funded by Lord Rothermere. Much to the embarrassment of the RAF, it was considerably faster than the front-line fighter aircraft of the day. As a result, Lord Rothermere kindly donated the project to the nation. Designer Frank Barnwell was tasked with adapting the aircraft to military purposes. It was initially conceived as a light bomber but was also taken on strength to Fighter Command to replace the dated Hawker Demon. At that time, the Air Ministry had a strong belief in the need for a turreted fighter.

There is only one surviving Blenheim in the UK – G-BPIV, a composite of a few airframes – which takes the identity L6739 from its nose section. After a landing accident in 2003, it was decided to return the aircraft back to its Mk I configuration, using a nose section that had been converted into a car just after the war. L6739 is a true Battle of Britain veteran and operated as a night-fighter until it was damaged in December 1940.

Following on from the First World War, the turreted fighter was considered by many to be a critical part of the Royal Air Force. Air Chief Marshal Hugh Dowding did not see the merits of such a machine but, nevertheless, the Air Ministry felt it important to replace the ageing Hawker Demons. In 1938, the Boulton Paul Defiant was the obvious and preferred choice, but the plane would not be available in the numbers required within a satisfactory timescale. The Blenheim bombers were, therefore, converted to Mk I(f) fighters.

In May 1987, the first airworthy restored Blenheim took to the skies in the UK, only to be destroyed in an accident one month later. It took another 5 years to restore its replacement airframe, which flew once more in 1993. After ten years of successful air show performances, this too was badly damaged in a landing accident at Duxford. The subsequent repair and restoration to the Mk I configuration was completed by the Aircraft Restoration Company which still operates the Blenheim today. In November 2014, the chief pilot and engineer, John Romain, took the unique aircraft for its maiden flight and it has been successfully flying ever since.

The Bristol Blenheim first entered RAF service in 1937 and by the time Britain declared war on Germany in 1939 there were well over one thousand in service. They were used for extensive bombing raids in the early part of the war and the Blenheim IV bombers continued to operate daily missions throughout the Battle of Britain. However, as a fighter, the Blenheim did not fare well, and early loses in the Battle of France ensured that the Blenheim Mk I(f) was only operated as a night-fighter during the Battle of Britain. Success was limited but not unheard of. For example, Pilot Officer M. J. Herrick shot down his first He 111 on the 4 September and scored a victory over another one ten days later.

The Aircraft Restorations Company's Blenheim taxies out as Supermarine Spitfire MH434 completes its display at IWM Duxford.

The Bristol Blenheim was ground-breaking in many respects – it was the RAF's first all-metal stress-skinned aeroplane. It also had a hydraulic retractable undercarriage, variable-pitch propeller and a powered gun-turret. At the time of its first flight it was faster than most front-line fighters, but the lead-up to war was a time for rapid development and the single-seater monoplane fighters would soon make the three-seater, Mercury-powered Blenheim obsolete and outclassed. However, as the first British aircraft to enter enemy territory on the first day of war, its place in history is sealed.

One of the Blenheim's most important features was its rigid airframe, which enabled it to take considerable punishment, leading to better chances of survival. Its robust structure also offered long life and gave opportunities for development and upgrade. Although it was quickly out-dated as both a fighter and a bomber, production would continue until June 1943.

Today's airworthy Bristol Blenheim often forms up with other aircraft, making up unique formations. Unsurprisingly, the only flying Blenheim is in high demand at air shows and is always popular with the crowd. L6739 can be seen here teaming up with an Avro Anson from BAE Systems heritage flight. The Anson is representing TX176, an aircraft based at RAF Coningsby during its operational career.

June 1940 saw an increase in night-time enemy activity over Britain. On the moonlit night of 18 June, over 70 He 111s raided Britain. Two squadrons equipped with the Blenheim were sent to tackle them. Incredibly, without the aid of onboard radar, seven crews were able to locate the enemy aircraft. Two were destroyed that night, but opening fire was risky business, as the light from the bullet trails would betray the position of the attacking aircraft – L1458 was shot down this way.

It would be two months before the night operations would repeat this relative success.

Similar design features can be seen between the Blenheim and the smaller monoplane fighters, such as the Hawker Hurricanes, seen here. It is also clear how technology had moved on in a short space of time. The lighter, single-crew fighters were ideal interceptors for daylight raids, but an extra pair of eyes was useful on night-time operations.

On 2 October 1940, in a desperate attempt to improve the performance of the flagging Blenheim, 64 aircraft were due to have their turrets removed. This modification would have given them an extra 80mph at the expense of some defensive armament. However, by this time the Beaufighter and more monoplane fighters, such as the Spitfire, were being produced in good numbers and the Blenheim could be relieved of some of its duties.

Billed as the *Battle of Britain Pair*, here the Blenheim is accompanied by a Supermarine Spitfire. This Spitfire is a much later two-seater training variant, a Mk T.IX also operated by the Aircraft Restoration Company. Although not a Battle of Britain aircraft, this Spitfire completed 20 operational sorties at the end of the Second World War. PV202 was built as a single seater in the Castle Bromwich factory in 1944, and was not converted to a two-seater trainer until 1950, when it went on to serve in the Irish Air Corp.

No. 604 Squadron's Blenheims were active on night-time operations throughout the majority of the Battle of Britain, where they could largely hold their own. On 11 August 1940, two of 604's Blenheims departed on a special midday operation, accompanied by three Spitfires. The detachment was vectored to a He 59 floatplane that had alighted 30 miles off the coast of France. The floatplane was surrounded by a few small vessels, an optimum target which the Blenheims soon had blazing. German fighters were soon called in to intercept, but the protection of the agile Spitfires ensured all aircraft returned safely.

A Bristol Blenheim is escorted by a Mk Ia Supermarine Spitfire (X4650).

The Bristol Blenheim is often escorted by several Spitfires as a showpiece at air shows. It is accompanied here by three Mk I Spitfires, echoing a scene from 1940.

By the end of September 1940, relief for the Bristol Blenheim I(f) started to arrive. The Bristol Beaufighter was set to be the RAF's first canon fighter, although modified Hurricanes would ultimately achieve this accolade. Beaufighters were a little late arriving to the Battle of Britain; the first aircraft were delivered in August 1940 and the first operational sortie took place on 18 September; by the end of October, no successful engagement had taken place. The Beaufighter would go on to serve the RAF, and other air arms, in various roles throughout the war but found its niche in long-range missions for Coastal Command.

There are two Beaufighters on display in the UK; one (RD253) can be seen at the RAF Museum in Hendon, whilst the other is on display at the National Museum of Flight near Edinburgh. The Fighter Collection at Duxford are currently undertaking a complex restoration of this aircraft (JM135), which is still awaiting a suitable Bristol Hercules engines to power it back to the skies.

A modern-day record of seven Hawker Hurricanes fly together in a typical early Battle of Britain formation at the Shuttleworth Military Air Show in 2019.

CHAPTER 6
FRONT-LINE FIGHTERS: HAWKER HURRICANE

The Hawker Hurricane's history can be traced back to the Hawker biplane fighters of the 1930s. Sydney Camm, Hawker's chief designer since 1925, had already developed successful biplane fighters for the RAF but felt he had maximised the potential that a biplane could offer. An advancement in technology meant that losing the top wing, which had previously been essential for structural support, was now possible and the potential of the monoplane could be unlocked.

Here, we see two examples of the Hurricane in formation. Both aircraft are based at Old Warden, Bedfordshire, and perform regularly at the Shuttleworth Collection air shows. The lead aircraft is a Canadian-built Sea Hurricane built after the Battle of Britain. P3717 at the rear was taken on RAF charge right in the middle of the Battle of Britain.

71

Sydney Camm took his idea of a new monoplane fighter to the Air Ministry, who were initially unconvinced. Nevertheless, with the backing of the Hawker board, Camm set to work on his new Fury monoplane, so called because of its lineage, which could be traced through the iconic biplane fighter. By 1934, the new design boasted an extra 80mph on its predecessors and heads began to turn at the Ministry. This speed was partly due to its new PV 12 Rolls-Royce engine, which would soon evolve into the world-beating Merlin. The prototype first flew in 1935 and became the first fighter anywhere in the world capable of over 300mph.

Four Hawker Hurricanes bask in the early morning sunlight as they prepare to perform at the Battle of Britain Air Show at Duxford in 2019. After the war, most Hurricanes were seen as surplus to requirements and scrapped. By 1951, when producers set about making the film *Angels One Five*, only two airworthy Hurricanes were available in the UK. Remarkably, the Hurricane has seen a resurgence in modern times.

On 3 June 1936, the Air Ministry contracted Hawker to build 600 Hurricanes, and the first production Hurricane, fitted with a more powerful Merlin II engine, made its first flight on 12 October 1937. By the end of 1937, Hurricanes were being delivered to the RAF, the first of these having fabric covered wings that were reported to blow out during high-speed flights. The first Hurricane pilots also reported their machine guns freezing at altitude. By 1939, all new Hurricanes were built with stressed-skin metal wings and heating units were fitted to the wings to overcome the teething troubles.

There are over 70 Hurricanes surviving throughout the world today, in various states of preservation, from crash remains to fully restored flyers. In the UK, there are ten that are currently airworthy, although thanks to the hard work of aircraft restorers such as Hawker Restorations, the number is increasing. After the war, many Hurricanes were disposed of and soon there were hardly any left flying. In 2019, the Shuttleworth Military Air Show saw a modern-day record of seven Hawker Hurricanes in formation together. A sight not seen for 70 years.

On 2 May 1940, a trial took place to compare the merits of the Hurricane against the qualities of its German adversary, the Me Bf 109. The initial climb rate and speed was better on the Bf 109, but the Hurricane was able to out-turn and remain on the tail of its German contemporary except in a steep dive. Alarmingly, Hurricane pilots had the tendency to black out when pulling out of a dive, but due to the reclined sitting position, this was not experienced in the Bf 109. Although the Bf 109 was a faster climber, the Hurricane still held the advantage in a climbing turn manoeuvre. The only significant recommendation from these trials was to paint the underside of the RAF aircraft duck-egg blue rather than the, somewhat easy to spot, black and white seen here.

Proof that the Hurricane was able to get the better of the Bf 109 on some level at least can be seen at the Imperial War Museum in Duxford. A 109E of the 4th *Staffel* of *Jagdgeschwader* 26 (4/JG26) was attacked by Hurricanes on 30 September 1940 and forced to make a belly landing in East Dean, Sussex. The aircraft is now displayed partially in the state it was found, with the other half of the wreckage restored to how it would have looked fresh off the production line.

At the beginning of the Battle of Britain, the main Hawker Hurricane in service was the mid-late production version of the Mk I, which featured an uprated Merlin III and a three-bladed variable pitch propeller. The later Mk I was armed with eight 0.303in Browning machine guns and the fuel tanks were given an extra layer of protection. By the late summer of 1940, Hurricanes were also fitted with IFF (Identification Friend or Foe) equipment, the aerial of which can be seen between the tail and fuselage on this image.

R4118 is a Mk I Hawker Hurricane that flew 49 operational missions during the Battle of Britain and shot down five enemy aircraft.

Pilot Officer Jock Muirhead took R4118 out for 12 of these sorties. On 24 September 1940, he shared the kill of a Dornier 215 with Pilot Officer Glowacki. Together, the two pilots took a number of sweeping passes at the German aircraft. Finally, Muirhead closed in to 100 yards from the stern and after a six-second burst of his machine guns, the port engine on the Dornier caught fire. Glowacki was able to take out the other engine whilst the Dornier was losing height. Four Bf 109s arrived on the scene and the formation was scattered. Sadly, Glowacki would not be seen again and Muirhead was also killed less than a month later.

Pilot Officer Archie Milne was also credited with a kill whilst flying R4118. On 27 September 1940, he was able to close in and take down an Me Bf 110 east of Dorking. Pilot Officer (later Wing Commander) Bob Foster would claim the most damage inflicted in R4118 after damaging two Ju 88s in September and shooting one down on 1 October 1940. On 22 October, Pilot Officer Ford took R4118 into action for the last time during the Battle of Britain. After a skirmish with some Bf 109s, he was forced to stagger back to Croydon, where the historic Hurricane was deemed beyond onsite repair.

In 1943, R4118 was shipped off to India to counteract a looming invasion from Japan. However, she was never required and was donated to Banaras Hindu University for engineering instruction in 1947. R4118 remained at the university in a forgotten corner until it was chanced upon by British business man, Peter Vacher, who eventually was able to return the Hurricane to the UK and restore it to flight.

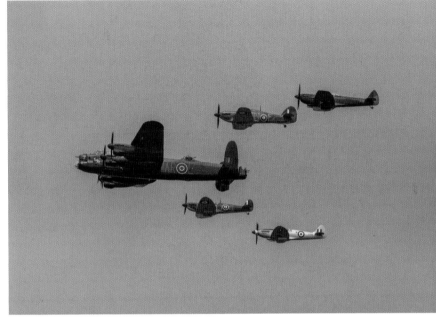

During the Battle of Britain, squadrons of fighter aircraft usually consisted of 12 aircraft that were split into two flights. Each flight was split further, into sections; A Flight consisted of three aircraft in yellow and red sections, whilst B Flight contained blue and green sections. Hawker Hurricane Mk I R4118 was operated by 605 Squadron during the Battle of Britain and often flew as the lead aircraft in the yellow section. It still wears its original colours from this period today.

R4118 would be flown by several other pilots, including Peter Douglas Thompson, who would go on to become a group captain and would

eventually form the Battle of Britain Memorial Flight (BBMF). Even immediately after the war, Thompson recognised that the heroic deeds of the Battle of Britain should not be forgotten. He decided to form a historic flight and took the only remaining Spitfires and Hurricanes available to set up his venture. To celebrate 60 years since its formation, the BBMF performed a display with the Avro Lancaster and four fighters in his honour – this was known as Thompson Flight.

As tensions grew across Europe, there was increased pressure on the Air Ministry to supply new modern monoplane fighters. As such, the Hawker Hurricane was rushed into production, a decision that would ensure an ample supply of the early marks ready for combat. However, the decision would ultimately cap the future design potential. Unlike the Spitfire, the Hurricane would be limited to just a handful of variants. During the Battle of Britain, only the Mk I and Mk IIa Hurricane saw action, the later aircraft having had the more powerful Merlin XX engine installed.

The Battle of Britain Memorial Flight operate two Hawker Hurricanes, both Mk IIc variants that were too late for the conflict in 1940 but were used during the filming of the *Battle of Britain* film in 1968; very few Hurricanes were left available by the time of filming. PZ865 was the last ever of 14,231 Hurricanes to be built and is pictured here in the colours of South East Asia Command (SEAC). This aircraft operated as a company test and communication aircraft for Hawker and was later flown in the King's Cup Air Race by Group Captain Peter Townsend, who had flown Hurricanes during the Battle of Britain.

Hawker's Hurricane was the most numerous aircraft in RAF service during the Battle of Britain; at any one point in 1940 there were well over 1,000 Hurricanes ready to protect the skies. Through the course of the battle, 1,994 were made available for active service. They conducted over 35,000 sorties, during which only 523 Hurricanes were written off. The Hurricane was also responsible for destroying more enemy aircraft than any other aeroplane. For this reason, many consider the Hurricane to be the aircraft that won the Battle of Britain, rather than the more famous Spitfire.

LF363 was built in 1944 and is pictured here wearing the Battle of Britain markings of JX-B from No. 1 Squadron, as flown by Arthur Clowes. The stripes on the wasp are supposed to represent the kills made by Clowes – his final total was 12 aircraft destroyed. LF363 was the last Hurricane to remain in service with the RAF. Following the war, it served on several station flights, including RAF Waterbeach, Middle Wallop and Odiham. It was a founding member of what is now known as the Battle of Britain Memorial Flight. Despite a crash landing in 1991, following an engine failure, LF363 is still flying today.

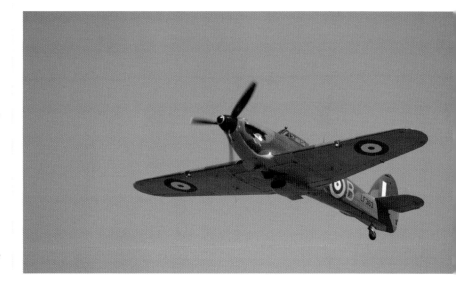

It is generally considered that the role of the Hurricane was to intercept the bombers, whilst the more agile Spitfire took care of the fighters. In combat, things did not work out this way. Hurricanes would often get embroiled in a dogfight with a Bf 109 or Bf 110 fighter as in the heat of battle, quite simply, the nearest RAF aircraft would be sent to deal with any would-be invaders. It is true that the Hurricane was more than a match for the German bombers such as the He 111, Ju 88 and Ju 87 *Stukas* but, providing the dogfight took place a low level, a well-flown Hurricane could take down a German fighter too.

An increasingly common site at air shows is a mock dogfight, or tail chase, between Allied and Axis aircraft. Here, a Hawker Hurricane is chased around the skies by a Hispano Buchón, the Spanish-built version of the Bf 109. Since its role in the 1969 *Battle of Britain* film, the Buchón has often been called upon to play this part. Genuine Battle of Britain period German aircraft are incredibly rare, but a handful of Buchóns have recently been restored and a 1939 Bf 109E (W.NR 3579) currently resides at the Biggin Hill Heritage Hangar.

Hawker Hurricane Mk I P3717 served with No. 253 Squadron at RAF Kenley from 29 August 1940 and joined the Battle of Britain at its peak. The aircraft was allocated to Pilot Officer W. M. C. Samolinski, who had served with the Czech Air Force earlier in the war. He escaped to Britain to continue the fight. Samolinski took P3717 up for the first time at 16:00 on 29 August on a sortie that proved uneventful.

On 30 August 1940, No. 253 Squadron were scrambled in the anticipation of a German attack on their home base, RAF Kenley. No attack materialised but the squadron, then part of the strategically crucial No. 11 Group, was vectored towards Brighton. En route, enemy aircraft were spotted and a savage dogfight broke out. Samolinski, flying P3717, scored a successful kill, a Messerschmitt Bf 110, but not without cost as P3717 was severely damaged. Samolinski was able to limp home but the aircraft would require extensive repairs. Less than a month later, the brave pilot was sent into action over the Channel flying a different Hurricane. He would never return.

Following on from its Battle of Britain skirmishes, P3717 was deemed so badly damaged that it was returned to Hawker in September for major repairs. Upon completion of the repairs, the aircraft was eventually allocated to the Soviet Air Force. It remained in Russia until the late 1990s, when it was recovered by Hugh Taylor who brought the aircraft home so that Hawker Restorations could revive the Hurricane and return it to its former glory. It first took to the skies again in March 2017 and is currently based at Old Warden Aerodrome.

Hawker Hurricane Mk I P2902 was built under contract by Gloster Aircraft in 1939. From May 1940, it joined No. 245 Squadron based at Drem, on the east coast of Scotland. There, it was engaged in shipping protection patrols. On 31 May 1940, carrying the code DX and R for 'Robert', P2902 headed for France to provide cover for the armada of small ships tasked with collecting the stranded allied army. Pilot Officer (later Squadron Leader) Kenneth McGlashan was at the controls. He engaged a Bf 109 but was badly injured. Despite this, he was able to make a crash landing on the beach of Dunkirk. He managed to return to the UK onboard the Thames paddle steamer, the *Golden Eagle*.

Over the years, what was left of P2902 disappeared from view and lay undisturbed until the substantially intact remains were rediscovered in 1989. Kenneth McGlashan, who survived the war, later commented on how his gentle landing on the beach was instrumental in saving enough of the aircraft to restore. In 1994, P2902 was registered as G-ROBT and in 2016, it was returned to flight in its original squadron markings by Hawker Restorations. It is currently owned and operated by Anglia Restorations and is based at Duxford.

Hawker Hurricane P3351 was built as a Mk I Hurricane, early in 1940. It served in both the Battle of France and the Battle of Britain. During the evacuation of France, P3351 served with No. 73 Squadron and took part in several defensive patrols. It was one of the last RAF aircraft to leave France on 7 June 1940, flown by Pilot Officer Peter Carter. During the Battle of Britain, the Hurricane joined No. 72 Squadron on 7 July but was damaged a little while later after Pilot Officer Alf Scott overshot the runway. After repairs, including a new engine, P3351 joined No. 32 Squadron where it was flown several times over the next few months by Pilot Officer Jack Rose.

of the Mk II with different levels of armament, more powerful Merlin engines and increased performance. From 1941, the Austin Motor Company in Birmingham was also drafted in to produce Hurricanes to assist the ever-expanding Hawker facilities at Brooklands.

After a brief spell with the American volunteers within the RAF (before the USA officially joined the war), P3351 was upgraded to a Mk IIa and sent to serve with the Soviet Air Force. It is believed that at some time in 1943, P3351 suffered a crash in the Soviet Union, where the wreckage remained until its recovery in 1991. With some initial work by Hawker Restorations, the restoration project was eventually completed on 12 January 2000 in New Zealand. A month later, P3351 was shipped to France and registered as F-AZXR. It has flown at several European events and air shows but is currently up for sale.

Production of the Hurricane continued at pace throughout the Battle of Britain and, indeed, most of the war. The Mk II series began to appear during the summer months of 1940. There were several versions

Hawker Hurricane Mk I V7497 was built mid-1940 at Langley near what is now Heathrow Airport, which at the time was little more than a small grass-strip airfield. V7497 was issued to No. 501 (County of Gloucester) Squadron and was delivered to RAF Kenley to make up for loses sustained during the campaign over the summer months of 1940. Like many aircraft of the period, its active service life was short. After just seven sorties, Pilot Officer E. B. Rogers, flying V7497 for the fifth time, was shot down by a Bf 109 over Kent on 28 September 1940. Fortunately, Rogers bailed out of the stricken aircraft and survived the incident. He also survived the war and went on to have a distinguished career in the RAF.

On 30 August 2018, Hawker Hurricane Mk I V7497 flew again for the first time, following a lengthy restoration. V7497 took to the skies once more in the hands of Stu Goldspink, who is without doubt one of the most experienced warbird pilots of the modern era. Hawker Restorations undertook what they describe as a 'nut and bolt' restoration, making sure that V7497 retains its authenticity whilst having that fresh from the factory look. The engine is an original Merlin III, also with Battle of Britain experience, having been recovered from a garden in Kent and painstakingly restored by Eye Tech Engineering in Suffolk.

P7300 is seen here with the authentically dressed *Spirit of Britain* re-enactors, who pay tribute to the heroic deeds of the Second World War. The scene is made even more chilling with the historic Duxford Aerodrome as its backdrop.

Hurricanes were also produced at other locations around the world. Yugoslavia and Belgium managed to produce some Hurricanes before their defeat, but the main source of overseas production was Canada. Canadian Car & Foundry (CC&F) produced over 1,400 Hurricanes throughout the war, many of which were shipped to Britain for use by the RAF.

The Hawker Hurricane currently operated by the Historic Aircraft Collection was built by CC&F in 1942. It was delivered to the Royal Canadian Air Force in 1943 and given the identity of 72036. Although it is technically a Mk XII model of Hurricane, it is currently painted as a Battle of Britain Mk I Hurricane. It pays tribute to the famous No. 303 Polish Squadron who shot down more aircraft during the Battle of Britain than any other outfit. The Hurricane proudly wears the markings of P3700, an aircraft flown by Sgt Kazimierz Wunsche. After sustaining damage in a dogfight with a Bf 109, Wunsche abandoned the aircraft over Beachy Head on 9 September 1940.

The Biggin Hill Heritage Hangar operate a Canadian-built Hurricane, which was built as a Mk I (later designated the Mk X) with a Packard-built Merlin engine. It was built as AE977 in the spring of 1940 but was briefly transferred to the RAF in September, before being converted to a Sea Hurricane for the Fleet Air Arm. It was written off in an accident in 1942, but after being recovered in 1960, and spending several years in storage, it was eventually returned to flight in June 2000. After a brief spell in the United States, AE977 returned to the UK in 2012 and was repainted as P2921, a No. 32 Squadron Hurricane that was based at its current home (Biggin Hill) during the Battle of Britain.

The Hurricane had proved itself during the Battle of Britain and it made up the largest part of the aerial force that defended the country. As the war progressed, the Hurricane would be developed to take on several roles within the RAF. The production of the more agile Spitfire hit its stride during the Battle of Britain, which allowed some experimentation with the rugged frame of the Hurricane. The relatively larger wings of the Hurricane (compared to the Spitfire) allowed for an ever-increasing armament, including cannons and small bombs, which led to its ultimate development as a heavily armed, menacing fighter-bomber.

AG287 was built in Canada in 1942 and served with the Royal Canadian Air Force for 12 months before being converted to a Mk XII, which was essentially a Mk IIb 'Hurri-bomber' with a Packard-built Merlin engine. It is currently painted in the markings of BE505 and can be seen here, ready to go, with model bombs showing what it would have looked like during the war. BE505 has recently been converted to the world's only two-seater Hurricane. Soon, passengers will be able to experience flights in a genuine Hawker Hurricane.

After the Battle of Britain, the Hawker Hurricane would begin to find new roles as a bomber-escort and ground-attack aircraft. The Hurricane was initially the main aircraft used to take the fight to the enemy, often escorting early bombers such as the Bristol Blenheim. These missions became known as 'Ramrods'.

Alongside an impressive array of nine UK airworthy Hurricanes, a further eight can currently be seen on display in British museums, including examples at both RAF Museum sites, the London Science Museum and the Thinktank in Birmingham. The Imperial War Museum, Duxford, also houses a Mk IIb Hurricane that was recovered from Russia in 1992. Its actual identity is not known, but it is painted to represent Z2315 of No. 111 Squadron with the markings it wore during the Battle of Britain.

The Hawker Hurricane was able to adapt to its new roles. As the Spitfire remained the primary interceptor, the Hurricane found use carrying out fighter sweeps that became known as 'Rhubarbs'. These were often undertaken by groups of four aircraft, which would patrol occupied territory looking for ground targets such as German road transport, railways, airfields and small-scale military installations. R4118, P2902, V7497 and P3700 are seen here in the box formation typical of that period.

Although they would continue to serve gallantly during the rest of the war, with their protection of Britain, Hawker Hurricanes had already earned their place in history. During the early stages of the battle, the Hurricanes were called upon to protect their own airfields and radar installations from German bombing, while later, they were there to protect the major cities as the Luftwaffe changed tactics. 1,720 Hurricanes took part in the Battle of Britain and they were responsible for well over half of the enemy aircraft shot down.

A 1938 Hillman Minx sits in front of a Mk I Hawker Hurricane, during the early stages of the Second World War. A number of civilian cars would have been requisitioned and repainted to serve in the RAF, with many being used by high-ranking officers, who would have been driven by a chauffeur from the Women's Auxiliary Airforce (WAAF). This car, which was taken into service in 1939, is in the bomb disposal markings of No. 15 Squadron. During the early stages of the Battle of Britain, attacks on airfields were frequent and the disposal of any unexploded weapons would have been a daily reality.

The Hawker Hurricane was much loved by its pilots, who praised it for its firepower and its ability to absorb punishment. It was the true workhorse of the Battle of Britain, and while it may not have had the glamour of the Spitfire, it was dependable, rugged and reliable. It was the RAF's first monoplane fighter and the first fighter to exceed 300mph. As the war progressed, the Hurricane may have been increasingly left behind, but in the summer of 1940 it was there when it was really needed.

Six airworthy Hawker Hurricanes sit together along the Duxford flight line. Due to recent restorations, sights like this are becoming more common at air shows. With several other projects in the pipeline, the record of seven Hurricanes flying together in modern times could soon be broken again.

Supermarine Spitfire Mk Ia N3200 takes to the skies at Duxford.

CHAPTER 7

FRONT-LINE FIGHTERS: SUPERMARINE SPITFIRE

There is something quite magical about the Supermarine Spitfire, with its sleek lines, elliptical wings and perfect contours that instantly draw the eye. The gorgeous hum of the Rolls-Royce Merlin engine on a summer's day immediately demands attention. There is also the mythology of the Spitfire too, and no other aircraft has achieved such legendary status in British culture. It has become synonymous with the Battle of Britain and represents hope, resilience and freedom. The Battle of Britain was just the beginning. The Spitfire would continue to serve for many years after the Second World War, with the RAF and other air arms around the world, and would be developed almost beyond recognition.

Supermarine Spitfire EE602 was built by Westland Aircraft in 1942. It is a Mk Vc variant that was developed after the Battle of Britain, so it has a more powerful engine, an increase in fire power and an improved propeller. Otherwise, it is visually similar to the Battle of Britain Spitfires. It is currently operated by the Biggin Hill Heritage Hangar. Part of the success of the Spitfire is due to its adaptability. It was developed into 24 different marks, with each mark being given a quantum leap in performance, allowing it to maintain front-line positions throughout the war, unlike the other Battle of Britain fighters.

The Spitfire was developed by R. J. Mitchell and the team at Supermarine and was based on their successful seaplane racers. The first flight took place in 1936, just four months after the Hurricane, but delays in early production meant that it was not available in the same numbers during the Battle of Britain. Most Spitfires in service during the battle were Mk Ias, armed with eight 0.303in Browning machine guns. There were also a small number of 20mm-cannon-armed Spitfires in operational service throughout the Battle of Britain, which were known as the Mk Ib. Towards the end of the summer the more powerful Mk II Spitfires started to replace the Mk I variants.

Seven Mk I Spitfires can currently be seen in the UK. Three of these are airworthy and the others are in museums. The RAF Museum have two, one at each location, whilst the Imperial War Museum and the Science Museum both keep one each on display in London. Here, we see X4650 and N3200 taking to the skies together.

Very early Mk I Spitfires were built with a two-blade fixed-pitch propeller, which was quickly upgraded to a three-blade de Havilland two-pitch version for later production models. Like the Hurricane, the early Spitfires experienced issues with the Merlin II engine and were also uprated to the Merlin III early on. The early Spitfires were capable of up to 367mph and had a range of around 300 miles, although changes in armament negatively affected this performance in some models.

Four Mk I Spitfires remain airworthy in the world today. One of these is now based in America, but for a short period of time all were together in the UK at the Imperial War Museum, Duxford.

The limited range of the early Spitfires meant that only 15 minutes of actual combat time could be expected with the engines at full power. The German fighters also experienced similar issues, with the added disadvantage of having to fly much further home following a skirmish. The Bf 109 Daimler Benz 601 engine had fuel injection, which enabled inverted flight. However, the carburettor-fed Spitfire would experience fuel starvation and the engine would cut out if this was attempted.

X4650, based at Duxford in the UK, is presently operated by Comanche Warbirds and currently wears its authentic No. 54 Squadron markings. Built as a Mk Ia in 1940, X4650 took its first flight on 23 October and joined No. 54 Squadron in Yorkshire a little too late for action in the Battle of Britain. On 28 December 1940, X4650 collided with another Spitfire during a dogfight practice. The pilot parachuted to safety, but the wrecked spitfire lay forgotten until its chance discovery in 1976. After a detailed restoration, the Spitfire flew again in 2010 and remains airworthy today.

The Spitfire first encountered enemy aircraft in October 1939, when two Ju 88s attacking British shipping were shot down. The first Bf 109s were destroyed by Spitfires in May 1940, but 67 Spitfires would be lost over France, mostly defending the Dunkirk beach evacuation from German bombers. For the Mk I Spitfire, the early missions over northern Europe certainly gave its pilots first-hand experience that would become invaluable when defending home turf.

During 2016, X4650 was given a temporary *Dunkirk* colour scheme to take part in the filming of the movie. X4650 became R9612 with the fictitious squadron markings 'LC' that were not actual codes worn by any Spitfires during the evacuation.

At the beginning of the war, Germany could build three Bf 109s in the time it took to build one Spitfire. Issues at the Eastleigh Supermarine works and the new shadow factory in Castle Bromwich, Birmingham, caused major delays in production. In May 1940, Lord Beaverbrook became Minister for Aircraft Production and re-organised the production lines and slowly, but surely, turned the factories into successful Spitfire production outfits. By August 1940, 18 Spitfire squadrons were operational in RAF service, considerably fewer than the 29 squadrons of Hurricanes available at the time.

Supermarine Spitfire AR213 is currently painted to represent a No. 71 Eagle Squadron machine, P7308. AR213 was built in 1941 and mainly used for training duties, as other marks of Spitfire became available at that time. After suffering a landing accident, AR213 was struck off charge but would eventually be made airworthy again to appear in the *Battle of Britain* film.

At the start of the Battle of Britain, Air Chief Marshal Hugh Dowding had just over 200 Spitfires at his disposal, while the Luftwaffe had almost 2,500 warplanes ready to attack. To many, the situation looked bleak, though throughout the first few weeks of July the Luftwaffe attacks were relatively sparse. Spitfire patrols scored a few early victories over some lumbering German bombers, but the relative inexperience of some RAF pilots and out-dated tactics gave the German fighters an advantage.

Spitfire AR213 has been given a number of different paint schemes throughout its long and varied post-war flying career, which includes air racing and air displays for several different owners. In 2016, AR213 became R9632 for the *Dunkirk* film but is now painted as P7308, an aircraft that still exists in the American Air Museum despite seeing extensive service during the Second World War.

In July 1940, 115 aircraft were lost and over 500 sorties a day was proving exhausting for the remaining pilots. A few early victories for the Spitfire pilots gave some hope, but the constant attacks on the airfields were destroying aircraft on the ground as well as in the air. The British radar and Observer Corps systems gave some relief to the RAF, by giving an early warning of attacks. This allowed the defending fighters to get airborne slightly ahead of the enemy's imminent arrival. The significance of these systems was initially underestimated by the Luftwaffe, who failed to grasp why the RAF were always ready to greet them.

Built at the Supermarine factory in Southampton in 1939 as a Spitfire Mk Ia, N3200 entered No. 19 Squadron, based at Duxford, in April 1940. Operation *Dynamo* was the mission to save the stranded British Army from certain defeat in France. N3200 was despatched as part of this operation on 26 May 1940. It was piloted by Squadron Leader Geoffrey Stephenson who led No. 19 Squadron on a sortie to cover the beaches as the army prepared for evacuation. On N3200's one and only mission, Stephenson shot down a Ju 87 before being forced to make a crash landing on a Calais beach himself. Stephenson survived the landing but was taken prisoner and would remain as such for the rest of the war.

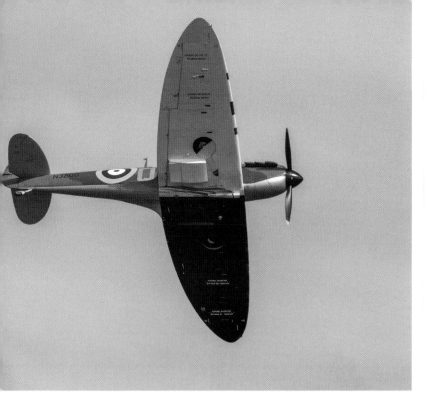

On 13 August 1940, the Luftwaffe finally launched Eagle Day, ten weeks after the Dunkirk evacuation. The delay between battles had given the RAF chance to re-group and gain some experience in defending the skies over Britain against the smaller attacks from Germany. On Eagle Day, hundreds of Luftwaffe bombers and fighters were sent in waves, targeting airfields in the South East. The RAF were able to break up the attacks, destroying around 50 aircraft and damaging a further 40. In return, only 13 RAF fighters were shot down. The Luftwaffe expected a decisive victory on this day, but RAF defences held firm, and many consider this to be a turning point in the conflict.

After spending most of the war as a prisoner, Squadron Leader Geoffrey Stephenson would continue his RAF career until he was killed in a test flight accident in 1954. His wartime Spitfire would remain on the beach in Northern France for almost 50 years before it was revealed by strong currents and excavated. N3200 was restored to flying condition through an extensive restoration programme, which was detailed in a Channel 4 Guy Martin documentary. It first flew again in 2014 and in 2015 it was donated to the IWM, where it is now on display in the very same hangar in which it was kept during the war.

K9942 is the oldest surviving Spitfire anywhere in the world. It took its first flight on 21 April 1939 and was allocated to No. 72 Squadron before the outbreak of war. It took part in several patrols through the remainder of 1939 and the beginning of 1940, though for K9942 most of these proved uneventful. K9942 saw extensive action over Northern France at the start of Operation *Dynamo* but landed wheels up on 5 June 1940, which in effect saw an end to its operational career.

After use in training activities for the rest of the war, K9942 was considered for use in the *Battle of Britain* film, but instead was chosen for several static displays at various locations across the country, until being donated to the RAF Museum in 1998. K9942 is currently on display at the RAF Museum in Cosford and appears alongside an array of both Allied and Axis aircraft from the Second World War.

Supermarine Spitfire Mk Ia P9374 arrived at No. 92 Squadron, based at RAF Croydon, on 6 March 1940. It is known to have been flown by at least eight different pilots, but Pilot Officer Williams was the first to achieve a kill in it, when he claimed a Me 110 destroyed over the French coast on 23 May 1940. The following day, Flying Officer Peter Cazenove would take the Spitfire over France for the first and last time; after just over 30 minutes of flight time, he was forced to make a belly landing on a French beach.

Cazenove was taken as a prisoner of war and after several escape attempts was moved to Stalag Luft III and became integral in the plot that became the Great Escape. Due to his size, Cazenove did not attempt to escape through the tunnels, but did help with forging documents for the escapees. Meanwhile, his Spitfire remained on the beach until its recovery in 1980. It was eventually restored by Airframe Assemblies on the Isle of Wight and the Aircraft Restoration Company at Duxford.

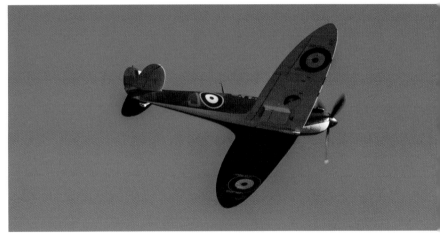

The first post-restoration flight took place in September 2011 and the Spitfire remained in the UK for a few years before being sold to an American owner for a reported £3.1 million in 2015.

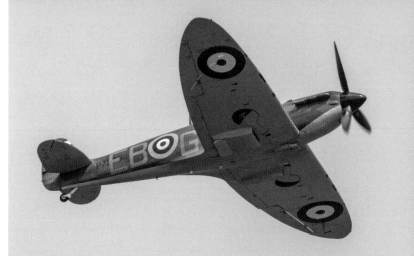

Supermarine Spitfire Mk IIa P7350 is the only airworthy Spitfire anywhere in the world to have fought in the Battle of Britain. It is thought to be the 14th aircraft built at Castle Bromwich and was given its first flight by the famous test pilot, Alex Henshaw. P7350 entered RAF service in August 1940 and was first issued to No. 266 Squadron on 6 September 1940. Its stay there was short and when the squadron reverted to the Mk I, P7350 was transferred to No. 603 (City of Edinburgh) Squadron on 17 October.

P7350 is currently operated by the RAF Battle of Britain Memorial Flight. During its time with the flight it has worn several colours, including the markings of N3162 EB-G of No. 41 Squadron, which it wore from 2011 until 2017. N3162 EB-G was flown by Battle of Britain Ace, Eric Lock, who, while flying this machine on 5 September 1940, shot down two He 111s and two Bf 109s and claimed a probable for a third Bf 109, thus becoming an ace on only his second day of combat. Sadly, Lock and his aircraft went missing on 3 August 1941 and were never seen again. He amassed 26 confirmed kills in his short career.

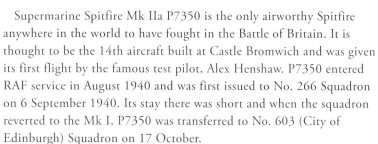

During October 1940, the fighting was still very intense, and operational service for most aircraft on the front line was often brief. P7350 was damaged in combat with a Bf 109 and forced to make a crash landing. Polish pilot Ludwig Martel was able to largely save the aircraft, but extensive repairs were required. Following these repairs, P7350 remained in storage for over a year before being returned to action for a few months in 1941. For the remainder of the war, P7350 was utilised in secondary roles, such as training and ground instruction.

During the 2017 season, in tribute to two surviving Battle of Britain pilots, P7350 was painted with Ken Wilkinson's code on the starboard side and Geoffrey Wellum's code on the port side. Geoffrey Wellum was the youngest pilot to fight in the Battle of Britain; at just 18 years old he was given the nickname 'Boy'. His 'QJ-G' code is visible here. Sadly, both veterans have since passed away.

A turning point came in the Battle of Britain when, in retaliation to RAF bombing raids over Germany, the Luftwaffe turned their attention away from airfields and towards the cities. When what became known as the blitz began, the airfields had a chance to recover, and the RAF was able to re-group and eventually mount more successful interceptions and return to a relatively undamaged base following a sortie. Had the Luftwaffe not switched targets, the outcome of the battle could have been very different.

In 1948, Spitfire P7350 was sold as scrap for £25, but the new owners saw fit to preserve the aircraft and donate it for static display with the RAF Colerne Collection. It remained there until its purchase for the *Battle of Britain* film in 1967, when it was returned to airworthy status and, following filming, donated to the Battle of Britain Memorial Flight. P7350 is currently painted in the markings of Al Deere's Kiwi III aircraft (R6895) which he flew 38 times before making a wheels-up landing. Al Deere was one of New Zealand's most famous pilots. Having fought during the Battle of Britain, he survived the war with an impressive record of 22 confirmed kills, ten probable kills and 18 damaged.

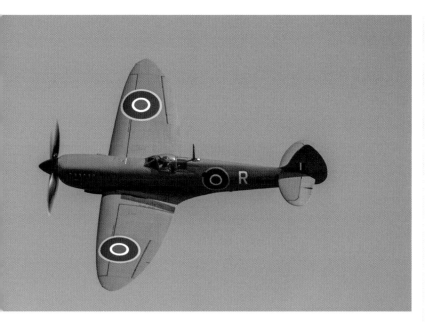

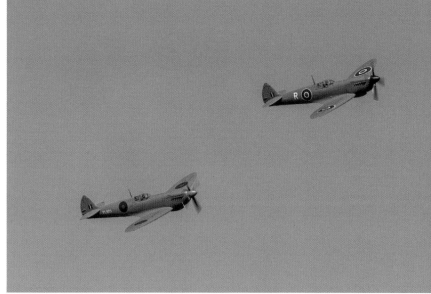

Not all spitfires were destined for front-line duties. From 1939, a small, but significant, number of Mk I Spitfires were taken from the production line and shipped to a former civilian reconnaissance unit that had been taken over by the RAF. In an operation led by Sidney Cotton at Heston Aerodrome, several spitfires were stripped of their guns and fitted with additional fuel tanks and large cameras. By the spring of 1940, modified Spitfires could reach Berlin and back in one four-and-a-half-hour trip.

No Photo Reconnaissance Spitfires from that period have survived but a few later models remain to represent the daring PR Spitfire missions flown during the war. Flying alone and unarmed deep into enemy territory was not for the faint-hearted. Fortunately, the adapted Spitfires were amongst the fastest aeroplanes of the time and were capable of flying at very high altitudes. Two Spitfire PR Mk XI are currently flying in the UK. PL965 is based at the former RAF Battle of Britain aerodrome, North Weald, and is operated by Peter Teichman. Spitfire PR XI PL983 is based at Duxford and operated by the Aircraft Restoration Company. The PR Mk XI was the fastest Merlin-engined Spitfire ever built.

The unique wing structure of the Spitfire allowed it to out-turn the slightly faster Bf 109. However, the differences were marginal and both sides were constantly looking for an advantage. By 1940, the Mk V Spitfire was being developed using a Mk II airframe with a Merlin 45 engine. It was considered a stopgap measure whilst the Mk III was undergoing a complete re-design. However, it became so successful that many more Mk Vs were built, and the Mk III never really materialised. The Mk V was a little too late for the Battle of Britain, but it would give the RAF an advantage for a brief period in 1941.

Supermarine Spitfire AR501 is an example of the Mk Vc, which is visually similar to the Battle of Britain marks of Spitfire in many respects, although this example has clipped wings. AR501 is owned and operated by the Shuttleworth Collection and is presently wearing its authentic No. 310 (Czech) Squadron markings. It was one of several Spitfires to be returned to the skies for the making of the *Battle of Britain* film. The close-up views show its authenticity; a few modern features have been added to the cockpit to ensure it can fly safely under today's regulations.

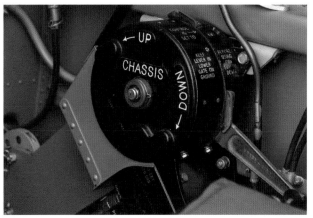

After the Battle of Britain, the Spitfire would continue to evolve as a result of the constant battle to try and better German technology. Each time the Luftwaffe would uprate or develop a new fighter, the Spitfire would be re-designed to match or exceed the performance of its German foe. In total, 24 marks of spitfire were produced, and each mark had numerous variants. The final Griffon-engined Spitfires were twice as heavy, twice as powerful and could climb 80% faster than the original Mk I built just ten years earlier.

There are various stories as to how the Spitfire got its name. Its fire-breathing start-up seems a likely inspiration, though it's also rumoured to be named after R. J. Mitchell's daughter who was 'his little spitfire'. MH434, seen here starting up its Merlin engine, is a Mk IXb Spitfire that was built in 1943. It was far too late to see action in the Battle of Britain but is one of the most famous Spitfires of all time, having a remarkable war record and equally impressive post-war career, including a starring role in many films and TV shows including the *Battle of Britain* film.

Although just a handful of Mk I and Mk II Spitfires remain, almost 240 different Spitfires survive worldwide to this day. Around 60 are airworthy, with half of these residing in the UK. There are also numerous examples in museums and several ongoing restoration projects mean that the numbers are likely to increase.

Large Spitfire formations are not uncommon as air shows and commentative flypasts are regularly able to gather considerable numbers of Spitfires in the UK. In this image, three Mk Ia Spitfires take to the sky in a mock scramble at Duxford Aerodrome, just as they would have done 80 years ago during the Battle of Britain.

Fifteen Supermarine Spitfires take to the skies in the
2019 Battle of Britain Air Show at Duxford.

CHAPTER 8
SUMMARY

The outcome of the Battle of Britain has been much debated. The German losses were considerable with over 2,500 aircrew killed or missing and a further 1,000 taken prisoner. The Luftwaffe also lost 2,000 aircraft during the course of the battle. However, Fighter Command suffered too, with the loss of over 1,700 aircraft and 544 aircrew killed. The battle took its toll on both sides, but in terms of numbers the RAF certainly recorded a decisive victory.

The aim of the Luftwaffe was to destroy the RAF in the air and on the ground, but by the end of October, German missions over Britain were still met with resistance from the RAF. In the eyes of the Germans, the British forces were still intact. In reality, the pilots were exhausted, and they were running out of aircraft. However, the RAF had done enough to deter the invasion and, critically, the German war machine had been stopped in its tracks for the first time.

Hawker Hurricane Mk I P3717 tries to shake of Bf 109 *White Nine* (played by one of Air Leasing's Hispano Buchóns).

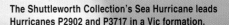
The Shuttleworth Collection's Sea Hurricane leads Hurricanes P2902 and P3717 in a Vic formation.

Much analysis of the Battle of Britain has taken place; the tactics, pilots, training, radar and aircraft have all been under the spotlight. The Germans seem to have had more experienced pilots and better aerial tactics at the start of the battle, but the RAF were quick to catch up. Differences between the single-seater fighters seem to be marginal but both Hurricanes and Spitfires had little trouble against the German bombers.

The 'Vee' or 'Vic' of three aircraft formation, with one aircraft in the lead and the other two on either flank, proved ineffective against the German 'Finger Four' or *Schwarm*. As a result, the RAF soon adopted the German formations to great effect. Here, the three Hurricanes demonstrate the Vic formation.

The *Spirit of Britain* re-enactors wait for a squadron scramble in front of Imperial War Museums' Supermarine Spitfire Mk Ia N3200.

Of the 3,000 allied pilots who took part in the conflict, 544 would give their lives. We cannot forget the sacrifices they made. Many were volunteers, and several had travelled from overseas to fight, including some whose countries had already been defeated by Nazi Germany.

Countless other personnel also contributed to this allied victory, using their skills in engineering, aircraft sporting, flight tracking and many other fields. Any aircraft preserved today are done so in honour of everyone who contributed; they will not be forgotten.

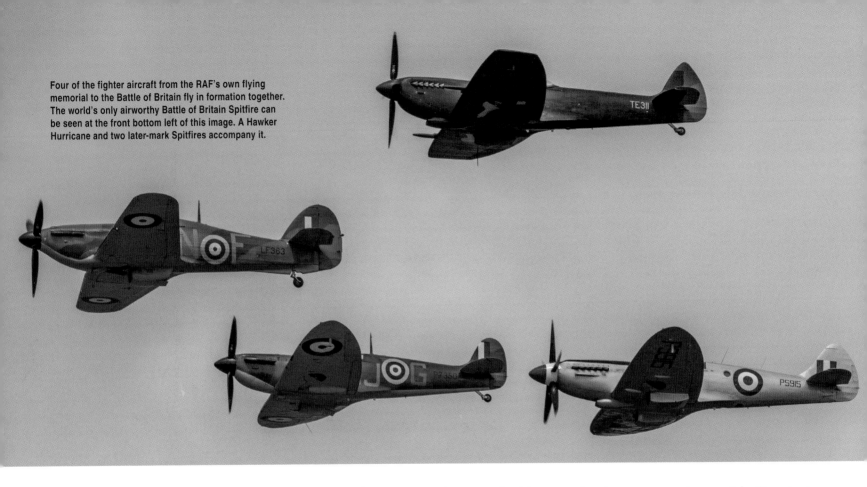

Four of the fighter aircraft from the RAF's own flying memorial to the Battle of Britain fly in formation together. The world's only airworthy Battle of Britain Spitfire can be seen at the front bottom left of this image. A Hawker Hurricane and two later-mark Spitfires accompany it.

Fortunately, several aircraft from the period have survived to help remind us of the heroic deeds of the Battle of Britain. Today, considerable time, money and effort goes into preserving historic aircraft. Air shows and commemorations take place so that these aircraft can be seen in the skies or up close in museums and memorials. Organisations such as the Battle of Britain Memorial Flight do sterling work to keep these aircraft in immaculate condition and ensure they will be there for many generations to come

The Bristol Blenheim stands outside at Duxford Aerodrome, and the Consolidated PB-Y Catalina can be seen in the background.

Throughout this book, effort has been taken to give a balanced view of the Battle of Britain aircraft and remember not just the glamourous fighters but also the aircraft that supported operations, trained aircrew and took the fight to Germany. After more than 80 years, unsurprisingly, some aircraft types are now extinct and as such have not featured in the book. The Second World War was a time of rapid development in the aircraft industry and as such aeroplane types became obsolete very quickly. Many civilian aircraft types were also impressed into service and, of course, the British Army and Royal Navy contributed significantly to the aerial battle, but that's another story.

To the public, the Supermarine Spitfire will be forever linked with the Battle of Britain, even though only the early marks took part. These aircraft are quite rare as survivors today. Several later variants survive and pay tribute to everything the Spitfire and its pilots achieved during the Second World War and beyond. Flights of multiple Spitfires are always a welcome sight and here nine fly in a diamond formation through Cambridgeshire's skies. There are no Battle of Britain aircraft in the formation as such, but for many it will be as close as we can get to the sights and sounds of the summer of 1940.

Supermarine Spitfire AR501 escorted by two Hurricanes.

Debates about which aircraft from the Battle of Britain were the best continue, and will carry on for many years to come. The Spitfire had the best performance amongst the RAF fighters, but the Hurricane certainly undertook most of the work during the conflict. The role of RAF bombing aircraft cannot be underestimated either as the bombing raids over Germany possibly influenced the Luftwaffe to divert their attention away from airfields, changing the tide of the Battle of Britain.

RAF Coastal Command patrol aircraft played their part too, locating the invaders and vectoring in the interceptors. The often-out-dated aircraft would even get entangled in dogfights themselves and, despite the odds, scored a few victories. Finally, without dependable and reliable training aircraft the pilots would not have had the necessary skills to defend Britain.

Eighty years later, the popularity of historic aircraft seems to be ever growing. The joy of watching a Spitfire, Hurricane or other historic aircraft perform remains. People are still left in awe by the performance of these aircraft; the speed, the agility and, of course, the sound. The purr of a Rolls-Royce Merlin engine stays with you forever. A ten-minute display can leave you emotional and breathless, as the aircraft go from a few fast passes to loops and turns, and of course no display would be complete without the final, poignant victory roll. The ever-expanding number of warbirds make for unique flypasts too, such as this formation of a Blenheim, two Mk I Spitfires and four Hurricanes.

Two Hawker Hurricanes sit as the sun goes down.

Getting up close to these marvels of engineering is an incredible experience, and the rapid changes in technology over such a condensed period are evident. The leap from a lumbering biplane to a 400mph sleek war machine in just a few years is mind-blowing. Thanks to the hard work of enthusiast, museum curators, warbird restorers and modern-day pilots, new generations will be able to witness these sights for many years to come. The memory of those involved in the Battle of Britain will live on – we will not forget the sacrifices of so few for so many.

BIBLIOGRAPHY

Beaver, Paul, *Spitfire Evolution* (Westminster, Paul Beaver & Beaver Ltd, 2016)

Bishop, Patrick, *Fighter Boys and Bomber Boys* (London, Williams Collins Books, 2017)

Blackah, Paul, Lowe, Malcolm V. & Blackah, Louise, *Hawker Hurricane: Owner's Workshop Manual* (Yeovil, Haynes Publishing, 2010)

Bowyer, Michael, *Aircraft for the Few: the RAF's Fighters and Bombers in 1940* (Yeovil, Patrick Stephens Ltd, 1991)

Brew, Alec, *Boulton Paul Defiant, An Illustrated History* (Stroud, Amberley Publishing, 2019)

Cotter, Jarrod, *Bristol Blenheim: Owner's Workshop Manual* (Yeovil, Haynes Publishing, 2015)

Dibbs, John, Holmes, Tony & Riley, Gordon, *Hurricane: Hawker's Fighter Legend* (Oxford, Osprey Publishing, 2017)

Dibbs, John & Holmes, Tony, *Spitfire: The Legend Lives On* (Oxford, Osprey Publishing, 2016)

Holmes, Tony (Editor) *Dogfight: The Greatest Air Duels of World War II* (Oxford, Osprey Publishing, 2011)

Lake, Jon, *Battle of Britain: Germany's Attempt to Win Air Supremacy over Britain, 1940* (London, Amber Books, 2000)

Mckay, Sinclair, *The Secret Life of Fighter Command: The Men and Women who Beat the Luftwaffe* (London, Autumn Press, 2015)

Nichol, John, *Spitfire* (London, Simon & Schuster UK Ltd, 2018)

Price, Alfred & Blackah, Paul, *Supermarine Spitfire: Owner's Workshop Manual* (Yeovil, Haynes Publishing, 2007)

Riley, Gordon, *Hawker Hurricane Survivors* (London, Grub Street, 2015)

Vacher, Peter, *Hurricane R4118 Revisited* (London, Grub Street, 2017)

Wilson, Keith, *Battle of Britain Memorial Flight: Operations Manual* (Yeovil, Haynes Publishing, 2015)